1998-1999
SMASH COUNTRY HITS

Contents

Project Manager: Carol Cuellar

FROM THIS MOMENT ON

Words and Music by
SHANIA TWAIN and R.J. LANGE

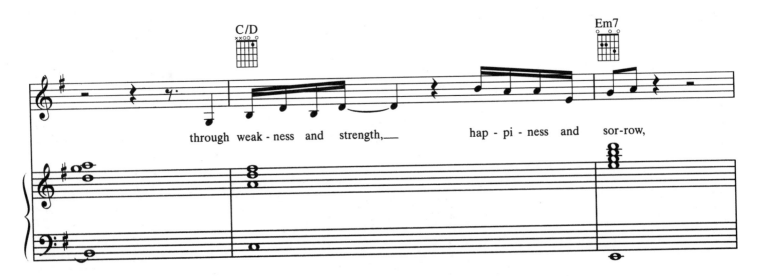

From This Moment On - 7 - 1

4

From This Moment On - 7 - 3

6

ing   I   would - n't   give,_____   from   this   mo - ment   on.__

You're the rea - son I__ be - lieve_ in

love._____   And you're the an - swer to___ my prayers_ from

Chorus:

IF YOU EVER HAVE FOREVER IN MIND

Words and Music by
VINCE GILL and TROY SEALS

Verse 2:
Music has ended, still you wanna dance.
I know that feeling, I can't take the chance.
You live for the moment; no future, no past.
I may be a fool to live by the rules.
I want it to last.
(To Chorus:)

ABSENCE OF THE HEART

Words and Music by
CHUCK JONES, DEANA CARTER
and CHRIS FARREN

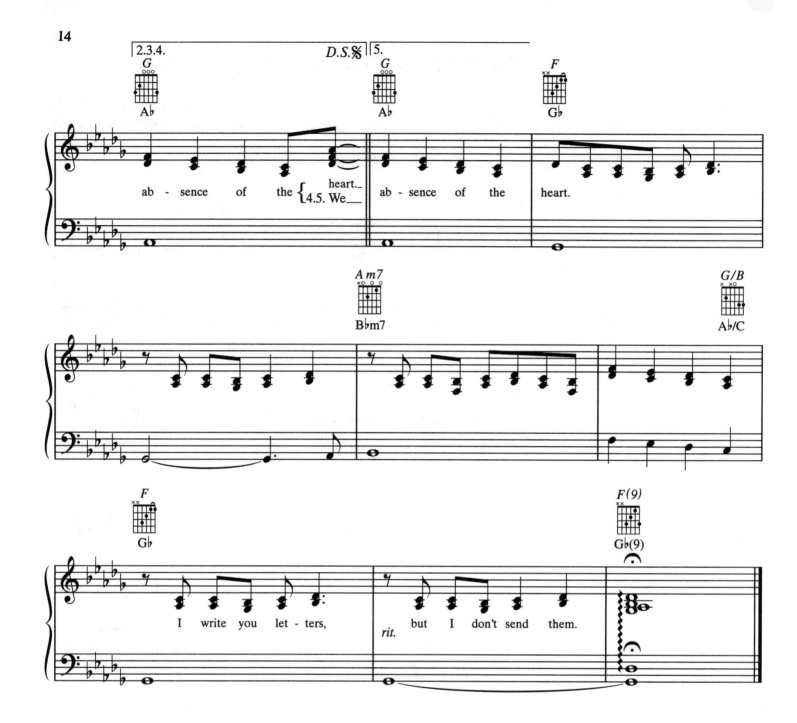

Verse 2:
How did we lose it?
Why did this happen?
When did we take it all for granted?
We sit in silence;
Inside we're cryin'.
How can we keep our love from dyin'?
(To Chorus:)

BURNIN' THE ROADHOUSE DOWN

Words and Music by
RICK CARNES and STEVE WARINER

Burnin' the Roadhouse Down - 5 - 1

* Optional Instrumental solo in cue notes.

Burnin' the Roadhouse Down - 5 - 3

BUSY MAN

Words and Music by
GEORGE TEREN
and BOB REGAN

Moderately fast ♩ = 80

1. There's a

Verse:

lit-tle boy out in the drive-way, his bas-ket-ball___ in hand, say-ing,
2.3.4. See additional lyrics

"Dad-dy, can we play a lit-tle one-on-one?"___ You pat him on the back and say, "Not now, son, I'm a

Busy Man - 4 - 1

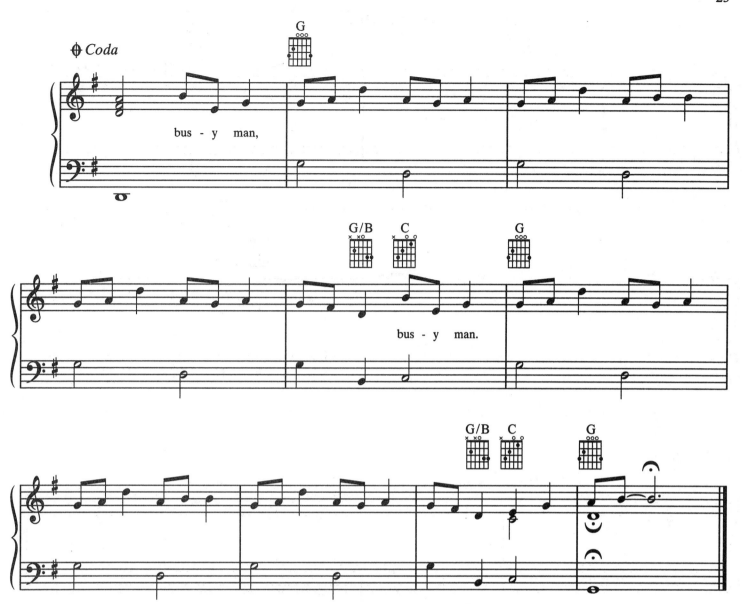

Verse 2:
His sister's out on the sidewalk,
Setting up a lemonade stand.
"Hey, Daddy, don't you want to buy a glass from me?"
You say, "Maybe later; can't you see I'm a busy man?"
(To Chorus 1:)

Verse 3:
There's a woman in the bedroom crying,
Saying, "I thought that we had plans."
You say, "Honey, I'm sorry, I'll make it up
When the job slows down and I'm not such a busy man."
(To Chorus 2:)

Verse 4:
There's a call one day from the office;
They need you down in Birmingham.
You say, "No way, the weekend's mine. I got
Plans with the kids and a date with my wife; I'm a busy man."
(To Chorus 3:)

Chorus 3:
You gotta go, gotta run, take a break and have some fun.
Those that love you most say you've come far.
Got some new priorities in that schedule that you keep.
And when you say that time's a-wasting,
Now you know how right you are, busy man.
(To Coda)

BY THE BOOK

Words and Music by
MICHAEL PETERSON and ROBERT ELLIS ORRALL

26

Repeat ad lib. and fade

Verse 2:
If I'd opened this book more often,
Then I wouldn't have forgotten
How much she cared.
And how much I meant my solemn vow
To honor, to have and hold her.
But as I read them over,
I know it's too late to say I'm sorry now.
(To Chorus:)

COVER YOU IN KISSES

Words and Music by
JESS BROWN, JERRY KILGORE
and BRETT JONES

Tune guitar down 1/2 step

Verse 2:
Baby, keep that fire burning;
Pour a glass of that sweet wine.
Let your hair down on your shoulders,
And I'll be there just in time.
(To Chorus:)

DON'T LAUGH AT ME

Words and Music by
STEVE SESKIN and ALLEN SHAMBLIN

FLY (THE ANGEL SONG)

Words and Music by
RORY MICHAEL BOURKE
and STEVE WILKINSON

Fly (The Angel Song) - 4 - 1

Verses 2 & 3:

Chorus:

FOR YOU I WILL

Words and Music by
TONY MARTIN and MARK NESLER

For You I Will - 4 - 1

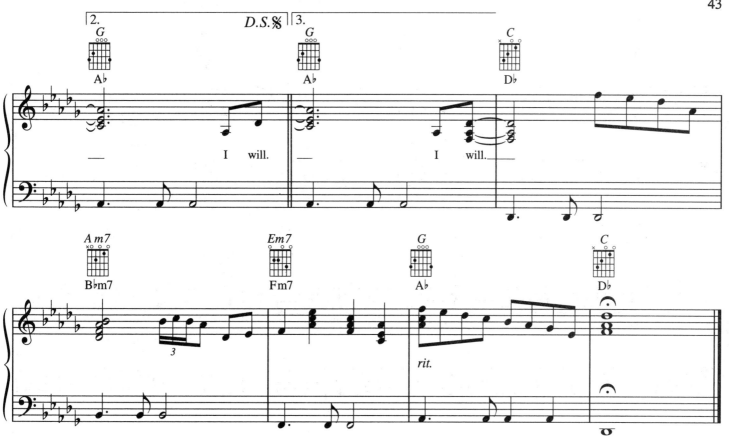

Verse 2:
It's not like me at all, to talk about
The likelihood of finally settling down.
Couldn't speak the words "I love you,"
Or find the courage to say "I do."
(To Chorus:)

HOLES IN THE FLOOR OF HEAVEN

Words and Music by
STEVE WARINER and BILLY KIRSCH

Verse 2:
Seasons come and seasons go,
Nothing stays the same.
I grew up, fell in love,
Met a girl who took my name.
Year by year we made a life
In this sleepy, little town.
I thought we'd grow old together.
Lord, I sure do miss her now.
(To Chorus:)

Verse 3:
Well, my little girl is twenty-three,
I walk her down the aisle.
It's a shame her mom can't be here now
To see her lovely smile.
They throw the rice, I catch her eye
As the rain starts coming down.
She takes my hand, says, "Daddy, don't be sad,
'Cause I know Mama's watching now."
(To Chorus:)

HONEY, I'M HOME

Words and Music by
SHANIA TWAIN and R.J. LANGE

Moderate country rock ♩=72

Verse 1:

1. The car won't start, it's

fall-ing a-part.__ I was late for work__ and the boss got smart. My

Honey, I'm Home - 6 - 1

52

Verse 3:
I broke a nail opening the mail.
I cursed out loud 'cause it hurt like hell.
This job's a pain, it's so mundane.
It sure don't stimulate my brain.
This job ain't worth the pay.
Can't wait till the end of the day.
Hey, honey, I'm on my way.
Hey! (Hey!) Hey! (Hey!)
Hey! Hey! Hey!
(To Chorus:)

HOW DO YOU SLEEP AT NIGHT

Words and Music by
JERRY SALLEY and JIM McBRIDE

The ghost of bro - ken prom - is - es___ you made___ haunts ev - 'ry room.

A hurt - in' heart___ can't get___ no rest___ 'round here.

I lie a - wake___ and won -

der___ how your con - science can___ be clear.___

𝄋 *Chorus:*

How do you sleep___ at night?___ Do you toss___ and turn___ till the morn -

Verse 2:
Now, your side of the bed's as cold
As the lies that I believed.
I'm at the point where I can't even
Trust you in my dreams.
Did the way you left me
Leave you feeling proud,
Or does the loneliness come calling
When the sun goes down?
(To Chorus:)

HOW DO YOU FALL IN LOVE

Words and Music by
RANDY OWEN, TEDDY GENTRY
and GREG FOWLER

60

How Do You Fall in Love - 4 - 3

I CAN STILL FEEL YOU

Words and Music by
KIM TRIBBLE and TAMMY HYLER

64

Oh,_____ I can still_____ feel you._ Yeah._____

Verse 2:
You said you'd love me forever,
Then you said it's over
And left me without the missing link.
I thought I'd forget you,
But I guess I forgot to,
And lately I've been too confused to think.
When I reach for someone new,
It's like I'm touching you.
(To Chorus:)

I'LL NEVER PASS THIS WAY AGAIN

Lyrics by
JACK MURPHY

Music by
FRANK WILDHORN

I'll Never Pass This Way Again - 5 - 1

nev - er pass this way, _ no, I'll nev - er pass _ this _ way, _

_ no, I'll nev - er pass this way, _

Freely
N.C.

a - gain. _

rit.

I'll Never Pass This Way Again - 5 - 5

I DO (CHERISH YOU)

Words and Music by
KEITH STEGALL and DAN HILL

* Original recording in F#.

I Do (Cherish You) - 4 - 1

Verse 2:
In my world before you,
I lived outside my emotions.
Didn't know where I was going
Till that day I found you.
How you opened my life
To a new paradise.

In a world torn by change,
Still, with all of my heart
Till my dying day...
(To Chorus:)

I Do (Cherish You) - 4 - 4

I WANNA FEEL THAT WAY AGAIN

Words and Music by
STEVE BOGARD, JEFF STEVENS
and DANNI LEIGH

I Wanna Feel That Way Again - 4 - 1

Verse 2:
Holdin' hands, walkin' down a dirt road in the dark
And knowin' everything was right.
We would dance and talk about tomorrow;
Our lips would touch and set the night on fire.
Back then there was nothin' that we couldn't do,
Believin' that dreams come true.
(To Chorus:)

WRONG NIGHT

Words and Music by
JOSH LEO and RICK BOWLES

Wrong Night - 5 - 2

Verse 2:
I briefly resisted, but my heart insisted
It was gonna be giving in.
Hard as I was trying, there was no denying
Which one of us would win.
You came up beside me and asked if I'd be
Wantin' to have a dance.
Right then I knew this thing was out of my hands.
(To Chorus:)

IT'S YOUR SONG

Words and Music by
BENITA HILL
and PAM WOLFE

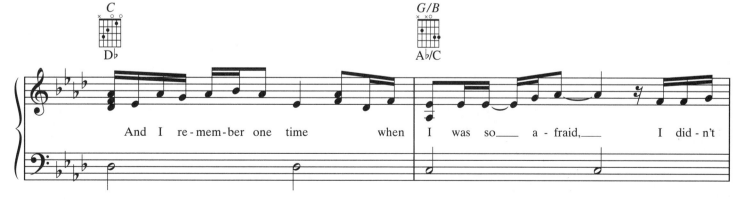

It's Your Song - 5 - 1

86

It's Your Song - 5 - 2

my heart to find_____ this place where I be - long._____ It was your_____ song.

It was your_____ song.

rit. It's al - ways been your_____ song.

freely

Verse 2:
Now every night I pray,
Before the music starts to play,
That I'll do my best
And I won't let you down.
And for all the times I've stood here,
This feeling feels brand new.
And anytime I doubt myself, I think of you.
(To Chorus:)

JUST TO HEAR YOU SAY THAT YOU LOVE ME

Words and Music by
DIANE WARREN

Just to Hear You Say That You Love Me - 5 - 1

93

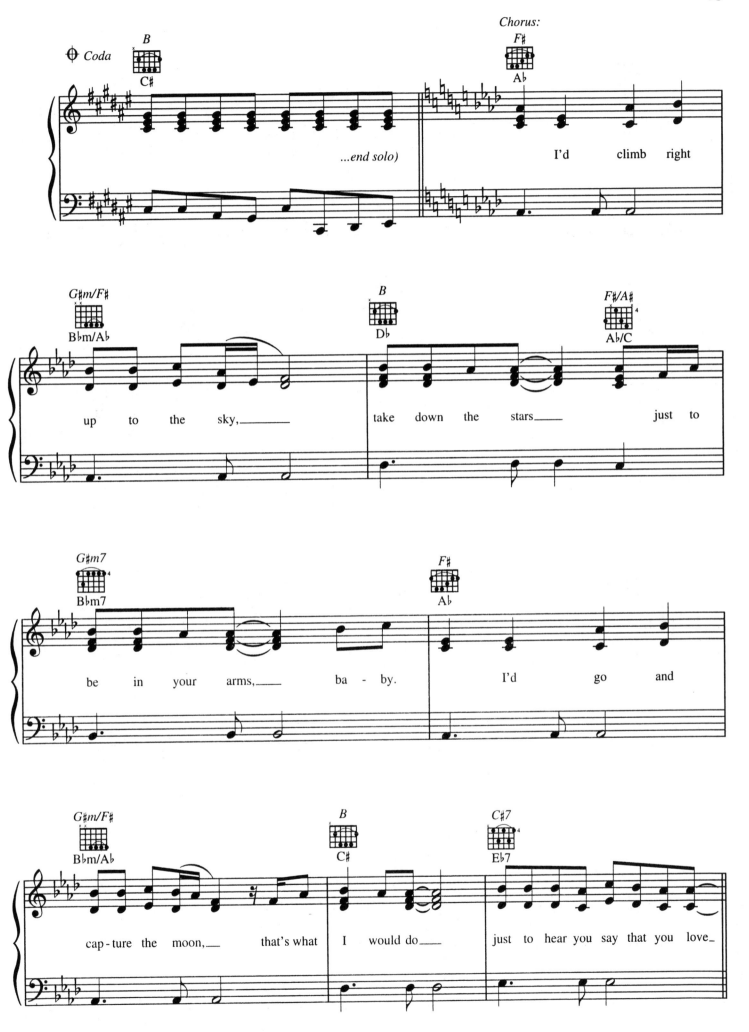

Just to Hear You Say That You Love Me - 5 - 4

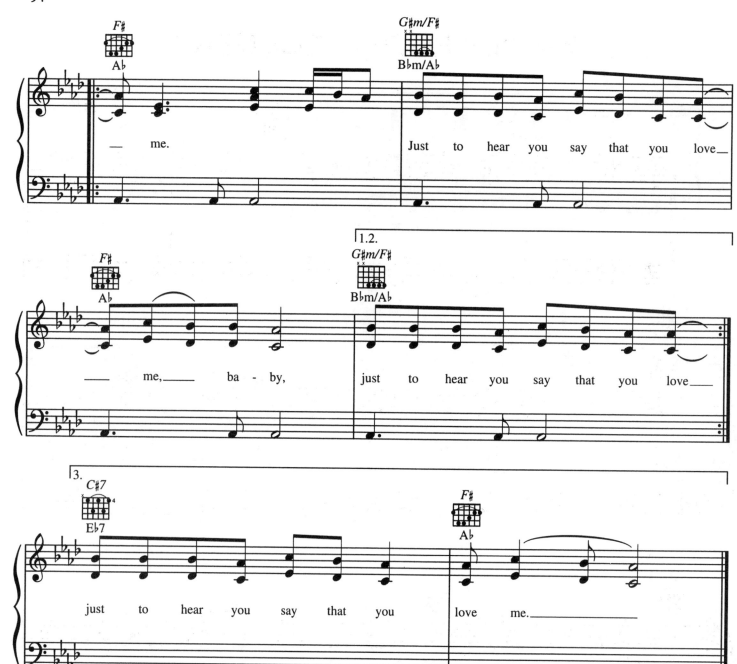

Verse 2:
If I could taste your kiss,
There'd be no sweeter gift heaven could offer, baby.
I want to be the one
Living to give you love.
I'd walk across this world just to be
Close to you, 'cos I want you close to me.
(To Chorus:)

KINDLY KEEP IT COUNTRY

Words and Music by
VINCE GILL

please play a sad song   'bout a heart that's just   been

stepped on.   Would you   kind - ly___ keep it   coun-try   for me   to-

night?   Would you   kind - ly___ keep   it

coun-try   for me   to - night?   *rit.*

LET ME LET GO

Words and Music by
DENNIS MORGAN and
STEVE DIAMOND

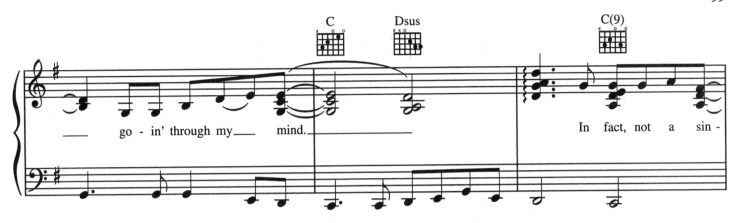

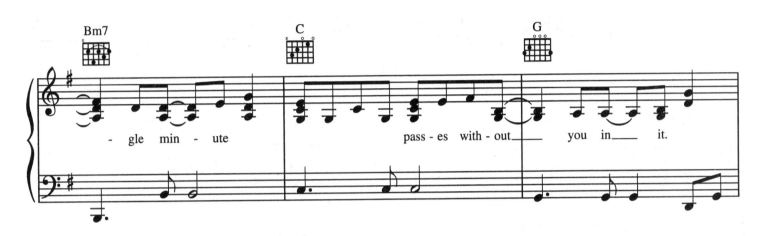

102

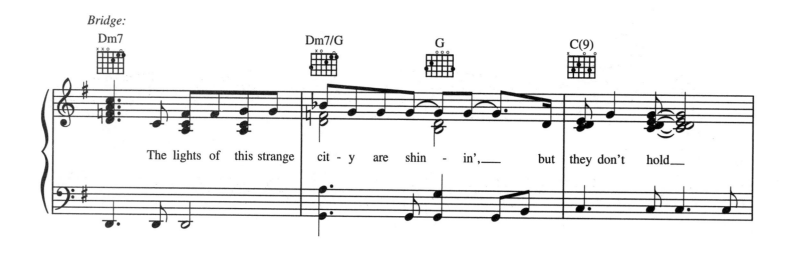

Let Me Let Go - 6 - 5

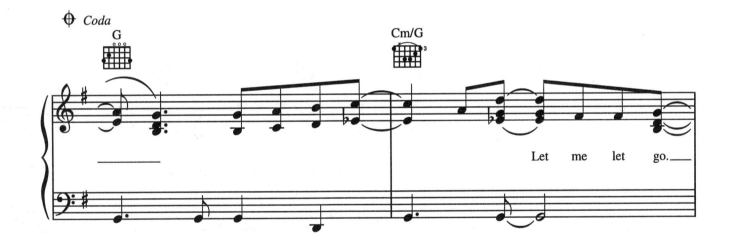

Let Me Let Go - 6 - 6

A LITTLE PAST LITTLE ROCK

Words and Music by
JESS BROWN, TONY LANE and BRETT JONES

long_ way from o - ver you.

2. These_ long_ way from o - ver you.___

I'm a lit-tle past___ Lit-tle Rock, but a long_ way_ from o - ver

you.

Repeat ad lib. and fade

Verse 2:
These headlights on the highway
Disappear into the dark.
And if I could have it my way,
I'd go back to where you are.
But I can't turn this thing around,
And nothin' short of breakin' down
Is gonna get me off this road I'm on.
I'm still a far cry from gone.
(To Chorus:)

LOOSEN UP MY STRINGS

Words and Music by
CLINT BLACK and HAYDEN NICHOLAS

Country rock ♩ = 128

110

Loosen Up My Strings - 5 - 3

Repeat ad lib. and fade

Verse 2:
Every night when the sun goes down,
You won't find me hangin' around.
I'm in loco-motion like a rock out on a roll.
I'm nobody's puppet. I'm out of control.
(To Chorus:)

NO PLACE THAT FAR

Words and Music by
TONY MARTIN, TOM SHAPIRO
and SARA EVANS

No Place That Far - 5 - 1

Chorus:

Chorus:

Baby, there's no place_____ that far.

rit.

rubato

rit.

Verse 2:
It wouldn't matter why we're apart;
Lonely miles or two stubborn hearts.
Nothin' short of God above
Could turn me away from your love.
I need you that much.
(To Chorus:)

A SOFT PLACE TO FALL

Words and Music by
ALLISON MOORER and GWIL OWEN

A Soft Place to Fall - 4 - 3

Verse 2:
Don't misunderstand me, baby, please.
I didn't mean to bring back memories.
You should have known the reason why I called.
I was looking for a soft place to fall.
(To Chorus:)

Verse 3:
Looking out your window at the dawn,
Baby, when you wake up, I'll be gone.
You're the one who taught me, after all,
How to find a soft place to fall.

SOMEBODY TO LOVE

Words and Music by
SUZY BOGGUSS, DOUG CRIDER
and MATRACA BERG

Somebody to Love - 4 - 1

124

Verse 2:
I've been to all of the places you go to,
And I've danced the tango with Casanova.
The wine and the roses are so continental,
But the champagne is flat and the tux is a rental.
All you want, all you really want...
(To Chorus:)

SOMEONE YOU USED TO KNOW

Words and Music by
TIM JOHNSON and RORY LEE

Someone You Used to Know - 4 - 1

Verse 2:
Bet you didn't tell him
'Bout that weekend at the coast,
Or how we used to argue
'Bout who loved who the most.
Well, I guess I won that one,
'Cause I still need you so,
But to you, I'm just
Someone you used to know.
(To Chorus:)

SPIRIT OF A BOY, WISDOM OF A MAN

Words and Music by
TREY BRUCE and GLENN BURTNICK

1. He was six -

Verse 2:
Hearts caught fire,
Love ran wild.
She cried the day
She called to say
She was having his child.
(To Chorus:)

Verse 4:
But tonight at a truck stop,
While drinking a cup,
The waitress grins
And winks at him
And says, "My shift's almost up."
(To Chorus:)

THERE YOU HAVE IT

Words and Music by
STEVE BOGARD and RICK GILES

There You Have It - 4 - 1

Verse 3:
This is confidential,
I've never told a soul.
Every time I see you,
I feel my heart begin to lose control.
And all I know
Is that I'm feelin' somethin' I've never felt.
I wanna be with you and nobody else.
(To Chorus:)

There You Have It - 4 - 4

THERE'S YOUR TROUBLE

Words and Music by
TIA SILLERS and MARK SELBY

should have been dif-f'rent, but it was-n't dif-f'rent, was the same old sto-ry, "Dear
2. *See additional lyrics*
(3.) trou - ble. *(Instrumental solo...*

There's Your Trouble - 4 - 1

Verse 2:
So, now you're thinking 'bout
All you're missing.
How deep you're sinking,
'Round and 'round, dragging down.
Why don't you cash in your chips?
Why don't you call it a loss?
Not such a big loss,
Chalk it up, better luck.
Could have been true love, but it wasn't.
It should all add up, but it doesn't.
(To Chorus:)

THIS KISS

Words and Music by
ROBIN LERNER, ANNIE ROBOFF
and BETH NIELSEN CHAPMAN

This Kiss - 4 - 1

TRUE

Words and Music by
JEFF STEVENS and
MARV GREEN

Moderate country rock ♩ = 116

1.True, in this mod-ern world when,
2. *See additional lyrics*

when two lov-ers get to-geth-er, chanc-es of 'em ev-er mak-in' it to for-ev-er

could-n't be bet-ter than two___ in a mil-lion hearts.

True - 4 - 1

Girl, this ain't just an-oth-er run-of-the-mill e-mo-tion,

what I'm feel-in' is the def-i-ni-tion of de-vo-tion, my love___ for you___

___ is true.___ *cresc.*

% *Chorus:*

True like the sun com-in' up each morn-in', bright as the light in a

mf

ba-by's smile.___ Sure as a moun-tain riv-er wind-in',

True - 4 - 2

right as the rain fall-in' from the sky.___ Girl, my love for you___ is___ true. true.___

Verse 2:
True, not another minute on this earth can be borrowed,
So there's no way to know when I'll live my last tomorrow.
But everyday I get, I'll share it with you.
This feelin' just keeps gettin' stronger as the time goes by.
It's written on my face, you can see it in my eyes,
My love for you is true.
(To Chorus:)

26¢

Words and Music by
STEVE WILKINSON and WILLIAM WALLACE

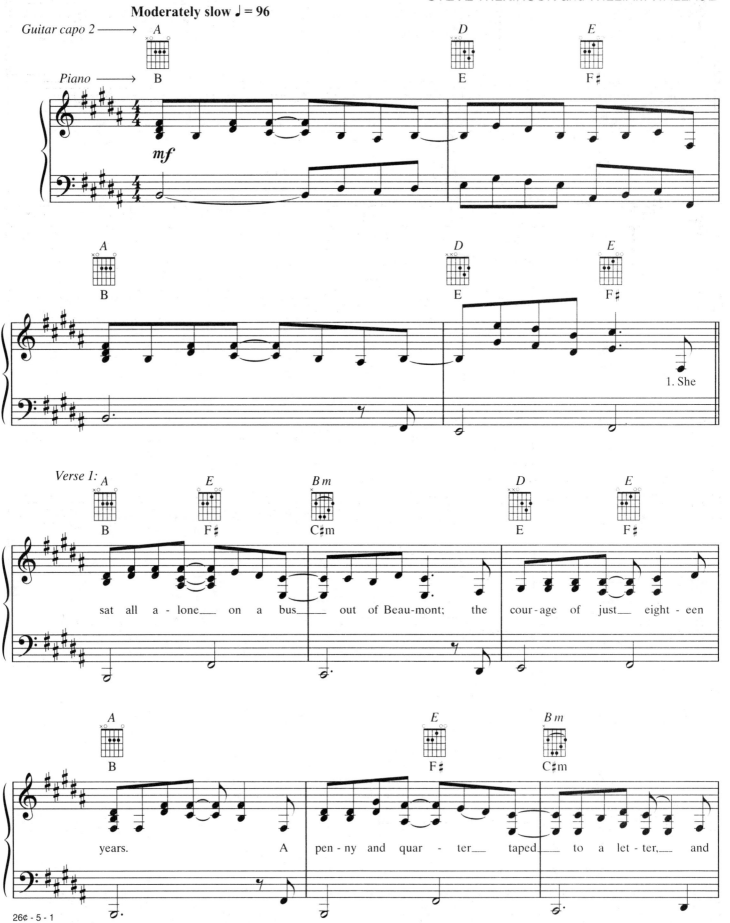

26¢ - 5 - 1

WHERE THE GREEN GRASS GROWS

Words and Music by
CRAIG WISEMAN and JESS LEARY

Verse 2:
I'm from a map dot,
A stop sign on a blacktop.
I caught the first bus I could hop from there.
But all of this glitter is getting dark,
There's concrete growing in the city park.
I don't know who my neighbors are,
There's bars on the corners and bars on my heart.
But . . .
(To Chorus:)

YOU'RE BEGINNING TO GET TO ME

Words and Music by
TOM SHAPIRO and AARON BARKER

You're Beginning to Get to Me - 4 - 1

Verse 2:
Got your picture up
On the dash of my new truck
So I can have you with me every road I'm on.
Babe, if what I feel is still
Just the tip of what I will,
I can only guess what I'll be like
When I'm completely gone.
(To Chorus:)

YOU'RE EASY ON THE EYES

Words and Music by
TOM SHAPIRO, CHRIS WATERS
and TERRI CLARK

Moderately fast ♩ = 120

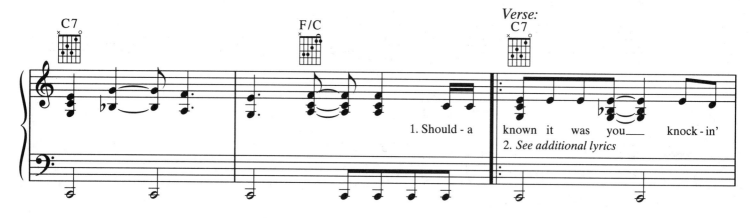

You're Easy on the Eyes - 4 - 1

Verse 2:
I got to admit, you got a smile
That really reeled me in for a while.
But it ain't funny, honey, what you put me through.
So why don't you send me your photograph?
It'd hurt a lot less than taking you back.
Then I could still have my favorite part of you.
(To Chorus:)

COMMITMENT

Words and Music by
TONY COLTON, TONY MARTY
and BOBBY WOOD

Commitment - 6 - 1

Commitment - 6 - 2

Verse 2:
What I'm searching for
Is a man who'll stand by me,
Who will walk through the fire
And be my flame in the night.
Oh, I won't settle for
Less than what I deserve,
A friend and a lover who will love me
For the rest of my life.
(To Chorus:)

Chorus 3:
Commitment, and everything that goes with it.
I need honor and love in my life
From somebody who's playing for keeps.
(Instrumental)

IT MUST BE LOVE

Words and Music by
CRAIG BICKHARDT and JACK SUNDRUD

It Must Be Love - 4 - 1

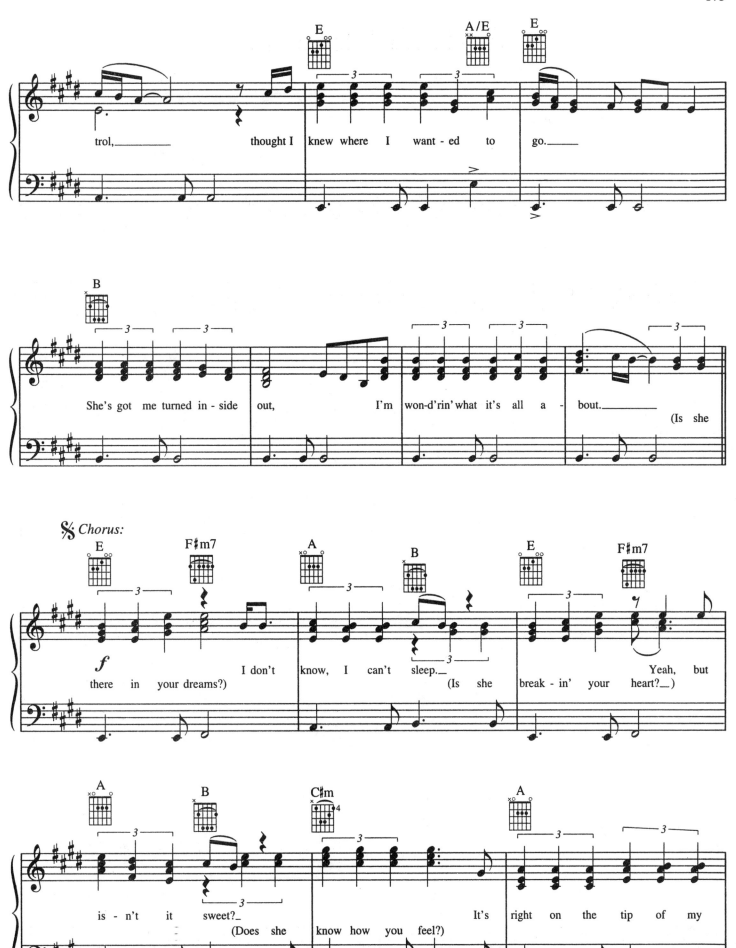

Verse 2:
I just missed my turn,
Guess I'm not thinking straight.
Oh, and what's with this car?
It's driving me back to her place.
I'm out here circling around;
I've already covered this ground.
These feelings just can't be denied,
So what am I trying to decide?
(To Chorus:)

The Best Personality Folios of 1998

JIM BRICKMAN—
Visions of Love
(PF9818) Piano Solos

GARTH BROOKS—
The Limited Series
(PF9823) Piano/Vocal/Chords

DAYS OF THE NEW—
Days of the New
(0230B) Authentic GUITAR-TAB Edition

CELINE DION—
Let's Talk About Love
(PF9813) Piano/Vocal/Chords

DREAM THEATER—
Falling into Infinity
(0209B) Authentic GUITAR-TAB Edition

FLEETWOOD MAC—
The Dance
(PF9742) Piano/Vocal/Chords

FLEETWOOD MAC—
Guitar Anthology Series
(PG9717) Authentic GUITAR-TAB Edition

GREEN DAY—
Nimrod
(0224C) Authentic GUITAR-TAB Edition

JEWEL—
Spirit
(PF9836) Piano/Vocal/Chords
(PG9810) Guitar/Vocal with Tablature

KORN—
Follow the Leader
(0308B) Authentic GUITAR-TAB Edition

MADONNA—
Ray of Light
(0263B) Piano/Vocal/Chords

JIMMY PAGE & ROBERT PLANT—
Walking into Clarksdale
(6385A) Guitar/Tab/Vocal

PANTERA—
Guitar Anthology Series
(0223B) Authentic GUITAR-TAB Edition

LEANN RIMES—
You Light Up My Life:
Inspirational Songs
(PF9737) Piano/Vocal/Chords

SEMISONIC—
Feeling Strangely Fine
(0284B) Authentic GUITAR-TAB Edition

SMASHING PUMPKINS—
Adore
(PG9802) Authentic GUITAR-TAB Edition

SHANIA TWAIN—
Come On Over
(PF9746) Piano/Vocal/Chords

VAN HALEN—3
(0258B) Authentic GUITAR-TAB Edition

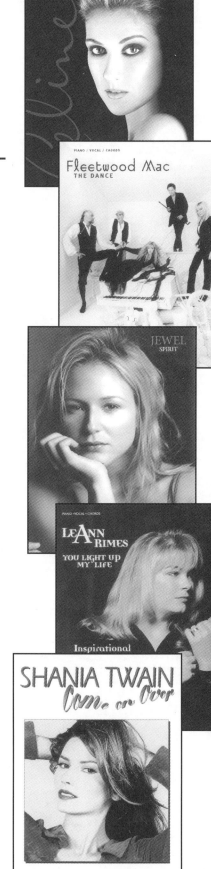

AD 0137

Showstoppers

100 or more titles in each volume of this Best-Selling Series!

Piano/Vocal/Chords:

20's, 30's, & 40's SHOWSTOPPERS
(F2865SMX)

100 nostalgic favorites include: Chattanooga Choo Choo • Pennsylvania 6-5000 • Blue Moon • Moonglow • My Blue Heaven • Ain't Misbehavin' • That Old Black Magic and more.

50's & 60's SHOWSTOPPERS
(F2864SMB)

Bop back to a simpler time and enjoy: Aquarius/Let the Sunshine In • (Sittin' On) The Dock of the Bay • Hey, Good Lookin' • Sunny • Johnny Angel and more.

70's & 80's SHOWSTOPPERS
P/V/C (F2863SME)
Easy Piano (F2863P2X)

100 pop songs from two decades. Titles include: Anything for You • Blue Bayou • Hungry Eyes • I Wanna Dance with Somebody (Who Loves Me) • If You Say My Eyes Are Beautiful • I'll Never Love This Way Again • Isn't She Lovely • Old Time Rock & Roll • When the Night Comes.

BIG NOTE PIANO SHOWSTOPPERS
Vol. 1 (F2871P3C)   Vol. 2 (F2918P3A)

Easy-to-read big note arrangements of 100 popular tunes include: Do You Want to Know a Secret? • If Ever You're in My Arms Again • Moon River • Over the Rainbow • Singin' in the Rain • You Light Up My Life • Theme from *Love Story*.

BROADWAY SHOWSTOPPERS
(F2878SMB)

100 great show tunes include: Ain't Misbehavin' • Almost Like Being in Love • Consider Yourself • Give My Regards to Broadway • Good Morning Starshine • Mood Indigo • Send in the Clowns • Tomorrow.

CHRISTMAS SHOWSTOPPERS
P/V/C (F2868SMA)
Easy Piano (F2924P2X)
Big Note (F2925P3X)

100 favorite holiday songs including: Sleigh Ride • Silver Bells • Deck the Halls • Have Yourself a Merry Little Christmas • Here Comes Santa Claus • Little Drummer Boy • Let It Snow! Let It Snow! Let It Snow!

CLASSICAL PIANO SHOWSTOPPERS
(F2872P9X)

100 classical intermediate piano solos include: Arioso • Bridal Chorus (from *Lohengrin*) • Clair de Lune • Fifth Symphony (Theme) • Minuet in G • Moonlight Sonata (1st Movement) • Polovetsian Dance (from *Prince Igor*) • The Swan • Wedding March (from *A Midsummer Night's Dream*).

COUNTRY SHOWSTOPPERS
(F2902SMC)

A fine collection of 101 favorite country classics and standards including: Cold, Cold Heart • For the Good Times • I'm So Lonesome I Could Cry • There's a Tear in My Beer • Young Country and more.

EASY GUITAR SHOWSTOPPERS
(F2934EGA)

100 guitar arrangements of new chart hits, old favorites, classics and solid gold songs. Includes melody, chords and lyrics for songs like: Didn't We • Love Theme from *St. Elmo's Fire* (For Just a Moment) • Out Here on My Own • Please Mr. Postman • Proud Mary • The Way He Makes Me Feel • With You I'm Born Again • You're the Inspiration.

EASY LISTENING SHOWSTOPPERS
(F3069SMX)

85 easy listening songs including popular favorites, standards, TV and movie selections like: After All (Love Theme from *Chances Are*) • From a Distance • The Greatest Love of All • Here We Are • Theme from *Ice Castles* (Through the Eyes of Love) • The Vows Go Unbroken (Always True to You) • You Are So Beautiful.

EASY ORGAN SHOWSTOPPERS
(F2873EOB)

100 great current hits and timeless standards in easy arrangements for organ include: After the Lovin' • Always and Forever • Come Saturday Morning • I Just Called to Say I Love You • Isn't She Lovely • On the Wings of Love • Up Where We Belong • You Light Up My Life.

EASY PIANO SHOWSTOPPERS
Vol. 1 (F2875P2D)   Vol. 2 (F2912P2C)

100 easy piano arrangements of familiar songs include: Alfie • Baby Elephant Walk • Classical Gas • Don't Cry Out Loud • Colour My World • The Pink Panther • I Honestly Love You.

JAZZ SHOWSTOPPERS
(F2953SMX)

101 standard jazz tunes including: Misty • Elmer's Tune • Birth of the Blues • It Don't Mean a Thing (If It Ain't Got That Swing).

MOVIE SHOWSTOPPERS
(F2866SMC)

100 songs from memorable motion pictures include: Axel F • Up Where We Belong • Speak Softly Love (from *The Godfather*) • The Entertainer • Fame • Nine to Five • Nobody Does It Better.

POPULAR PIANO SHOWSTOPPERS
(F2876P9B)

100 popular intermediate piano solos include: Baby Elephant Walk • Gonna Fly Now (Theme from *Rocky*) • The Hill Street Blues Theme • Love Is a Many-Splendored Thing • (Love Theme from) *Romeo and Juliet* • Separate Lives (Love Theme from *White Nights*) • The Shadow of Your Smile • Theme from *The Apartment* • Theme from *New York, New York*.

RAGTIME SHOWSTOPPERS
(F2867SMX)

These 100 original classic rags by Scott Joplin, James Scott, Joseph Lamb and other ragtime composers include: Maple Leaf Rag • The Entertainer • Kansas City Rag • Ma Rag Time Baby • The St. Louis Rag • World's Fair Rag and many others.

ROMANTIC SHOWSTOPPERS
(F2870SMC)

101 beautiful songs including: After All (Love Theme from *Chances Are*) • Here and Now • I Can't Stop Loving You • If You Say My Eyes Are Beautiful • The Vows Go Unbroken (Always True to You) • You Got It.

TELEVISION SHOWSTOPPERS
(F2874SMC)

103 TV themes including: Another World • Dear John • Hall or Nothing (The Arsenio Hall Show) • Star Trek -The Next Generation (Main Title) • Theme from "Cheers" (Where Everybody Knows Your Name).

BIGGEST
POP HITS & COUNTRY HITS
OF 1998

BIGGEST
POP HITS OF 1998

(MF9820) Piano/Vocal/Chords
(AF9835) Easy Piano arr. Coates & Brimhall

- The biggest songs from the hottest artists
- More than 30 hit songs
- Available in P/V/C and Easy Piano Editions

Titles (and artists) include: **I Don't Want to Miss a Thing** (Aerosmith) • **My Heart Will Go On** (Celine Dion) • **How Do I Live** (LeAnn Rimes) • **You're Still the One** (Shania Twain) • **Ray of Light** (Madonna) • **All My Life** (K-Ci & Jo Jo) • **Good Riddance (Time of Your Life)** (Green Day) • **This Kiss** (Faith Hill) • **Kiss the Rain** (Billie Myers) • **Walkin' on the Sun** (Smash Mouth) and many more.

BIGGEST
COUNTRY HITS OF 1998

(MF9819) Piano/Vocal/Chords

- The top country songs of the year
- The hottest country artists
- All of your favorites collected together in one great folio

Titles (and artists) include: **You're Still the One** (Shania Twain) • **This Kiss** (Faith Hill) • **Nothin' But the Taillights** (Clint Black) • **There's Your Trouble** (Dixie Chicks) • **How Do I Live** (LeAnn Rimes) • **From This Moment On** (Shania Twain & Bryan White) • **I Do (Cherish You)** (Mark Wills) • **Cover You in Kisses** (John Michael Montgomery) • **Bad Day to Let You Go** (Bryan White) • **Holes in the Floor of Heaven** (Steve Wariner) and many more.

AD 0138